The Residents

poems by

Matthew J. Friday

Finishing Line Press
Georgetown, Kentucky

The Residents

One does not travel to arrive,
but for the sake of the journey itself.
Johan Wolfgang von Goethe.

That the powerful play goes on,
and you may contribute a verse.
Walt Whitman.

ACKNOWLEDGMENTS

Poems from this collection have appeared in:

*Acta Victoriana (CA), Borderless Journal (India), Brushfire Literature & Arts Journal,
The Dawntreader (UK), Inlandia, The Journal (UK), Listeners Unite Anthology,
Lothlorien Poetry Journal, Lunch Ticket, The Oregon English Journal, Rathalla Review,
Shot Glass Journal, Sparks of Calliope, Verbal Art (India) and Willawaw Journal.*

"Against the Current" was nominated for the 2021 Pushcart Prize.

The Origami Poems Project published a micro-chap titled "The Resident" which
featured 6 poems from this collection.

Publisher: Leah Huete de Maines
Editor: Christen Kincaid
Cover Art and Design: Morgan Brown
Author Photo:Morgan Brown

Order online: www.finishinglinepress.com
also available on amazon.com

Author inquiries and mail orders:
Finishing Line Press
PO Box 1626
Georgetown, Kentucky 40324
USA

Contents

Arrival in America
With thanks to Emma Lazarus

No dirt cheap steerage ticket from Liverpool,
jammed in the hold of an empty cotton ship,
holding onto few belongings, threadbare coat,
stalked by typhus and seasickness, the sudden
spewing out onto Ellis Island, cross-examinations
by indifferent border guards, shaming medical
inspections, new names, compassion from former
immigrants, instant friends plotting to fleece.

My ship is a trans-Atlantic flight from Amsterdam.
in a half-price Economy— desperate airline—trying
to ignore the complaints of a wandering tempest,
coughing travelers lying flat to breathe freely,
unmasked protestors huddled in masses of denial.
I lower my mask only to gobble lukewarm dinner.
I keep my bag close, bulging with paperwork
and hopes that the Embassy's good wishes work.

A Customs Officer colossus fueled by viral fear.
He prescribes infectious orders and irritation.
Obedient and fearful, I accept the accusations
of mysterious forms not filled in, the dismissive
hand when I offer my paperwork (that will create
a Kafkaesque series of complications months later).
Hurried handwriting suggests dishonesty. 1-1000
-the chances of contracting the *British* variant.

I'm British but haven't been there for over a year.
He lowers his guard, risks a small smile, but still
warns me he could get sick. Desperate for humanity,
I tell him I understand his fear. His shoulders relax.
He stamps the passport and holds it out, warning me
not to get any trouble. I hurry away in my last pair
of shoes, torn on the inside. A Russian-American TSA
agent welcomes me with smiles and a warming story
about having an English wife. From Reading. One
short flight to Portland to meet my mighty woman.
Seattle shrinks below to the size of a concrete hive.
The line of Cascade volcanoes state in a wintry ellipse
amongst rugged sentences of hills, all named after
presidents, generals and diplomats replacing names
from native legends as old as glaciers. My wife waits
wearing a respirator by the golden Arrivals door.

Just Hunger

I run down to the sloping, sandy
yellow field, bumped by blackened
heaps of old snow. Here a swainson
hawk patrols, marking ley-lines with
sharp eyes, then watching them tremble
from atop a roadside telegraph pole.
Something new today: the shrubs
torn up and the frosted field marked
with little orange survey flags. His plot
bordered by a growing forest of blocks
and backyards: White Salmon town
spawning. Does he understand that
he has lost the land of his ancestors,
no recompense or apology, just hunger.

Let There Be Baked White Bread

After three failed attempts with my wife,
My father-in-law takes the mantle of teacher.
With the patience of a Biblical Father, He
teaches me to measure and mix the dough,
as precisely as a desperate prayer. The
mixture made, we must leave it overnight
to be blessed by warmth and the invisible.

The next day we inspect my first creation.
Bloated with the hot air of virgin hope,
we flour our hands and He guides me
to roll, prod, fold and form the mound.
The veined globe is ready for the fires,
so we reverentially prepare the oven
and place inside, closing with new psalms.

Thirty minutes later, there was light
and a lightly browned white bread loaf.
A sacrament of salt and olive oil to harden
the crust. Ten minutes later, the bread
was truly born and I held it aloft in mittens,
as proud as any Abraham. Knife in hand,
I'm ready to sacrifice all for my people.

Route 22 Memorial

On route 22 to Bend we pass Mill City and
the blasted heaths of last summer's fires,
so bad they closed Portland, millions muffled.

The road passes through blackened brigades
of Santiam Forest trees and piles of the fallen,
heaped up in snow-stained charnel clearances.

In vacated lots the rubble of homes linger,
indiscriminately chosen by the concentration,
a few ironic fireplaces and chimneys still standing.

Skeletal cars lay scattered like shells. Trailers
have multiplied. Blink and you might think tourists.
A few pristine houses escaped the fist of the fire.

The burnt skin of the hills with charcoaled trees
like my grandfather whose hair fell out during
World War Two's shock and North African heat.

The Santiam River slips past guiltily. We climb
towards the Willamette National Forest, soothing
rain becoming concerning snow. At Detroit Lake,

we find a European battlefield, blackened stumps
memorializing the mud. The dead cleared to create
a buffer zone. On one side of Detroit, a motel sign

hangs by the stony scar of itself. On the other side
the grocery store is still surviving. More rubble piles,
more sudden trailer living and lonely fireplaces.

Leaving we smell woodsmoke and see smoldering
signals that in the earth not all is forgotten, people
trying to live and not worry about next summer.

The Wind in the Pines Trees

My wife and I were exploring our suburb in Bend
on the fringe of town where houses squat between
boulders of igneous indifference rolled there before
any human knew cougar. An Olympian wind builds
above Mount Batchelor and charges down, all boast
and sleet. The pine sirens around us rustle and creak.
My wife tells me how much she likes the sounds,
how different a nectar it is from the deciduous wind
of our last home. I tie myself to the pines as they
resist movement, the evening, the passing furies.

Against the Current

The red-tailed hawk flies a tugged line
over the pines that rig the riverside,
along a taste of cracked toffee rocks.

Oddly slow, the hawk, as if fighting a tide.
Puppet wings but the strings are invisible.
Behind the river groans. There's a plan

to build 250 homes against the cliffs,
trees to be cleared, paths suffocated,
the hawk's clawed opinions ignored.

Devotee on the Deschutes

Here is poetry, Apollo winks,
on a warm March afternoon.
The constant river shredded
by rocks into a silk archipelago,
shimmering in sunlit stillness,
the music of immovable motion
shattered by a retriever wrecking
the river, threatening to shake
itself by me. Poetry paddles
away from another dog's soiling
bark and the empty commands
of owners. Apollo is laughing.
You are no Epsom Orpheus,
just a devotee on the Deschutes.

Kingfisher Gift

Elevated
on a trunk of petrified gray wood
near the bank of Deschutes River
is the belted kingfisher.

I watch from behind a pine tree.

The wind ruffles its accumulating crest.
It looks left and right,
scanning the shallow waters
for any hint or flick or wink.

I felt fortunate for
a few minutes of wings and pen,
so unfamiliar it felt tropical—
an Amazonian moment in Oregon.

I shuffled and shot the kingfisher
upstream on clangorous wings.
I was left bereft,
my blank page swirling.

Wordsworth in Bend

Not a Milky Way of flowers,
more a scattered cluster of stars

on the riverbank, dancing like they did
for Wordsworth, giddy in the near gale

that tears at the flags lining the Old Mill
bridge over the Deschutes River.

On the river ballets an early universe of
violent-green swallows in a chaos

of lines and loops, an ecstatic
bombardment of atomic bodies,

never colliding, always forming new
shapes over the ruffled water.

While there are daffodils and swallows
to recall when locked in concrete retreats

we have the same hope as Wordsworth.

April Frogs

April's cruelty is calmed
by the singing frogs.

Every evening they begin
I am reminded
                        of my smile.

Their bubbling boast of place
somewhere by the lava rocks

and the spewing houses
that pour into the space

between here and the river,
the stranded deer and deep

croaking that continues
as long as they can reach water.

Patience

So there you are osprey atop
a lightning clawed tree, shorn
at the top. There's the scruffy
egg of your home. You crack
on outstretched limb, as still
as a dreaming volcano, head
peaked with snow, the slightest
of turn in the feathered wind.
Below the tumble rocks stop,
and naked, cracked trunks lay
writing the river where heron
as gray as the current-cupped
stone unfolds quilled calligraphy
and congratulates my patience.

Easter Eggs

My father-in-law shows me the picture:
cupped in a perfectly woven crown,
two blue jewels, thickly speckled with hope.

We go outside to peer into the bush.
The mother watches from the tree.
Only a few seconds, so as not to spook her.

If only every person of faith and indecision
could look at the birds' nest
they would realize what matters.

The In-laws think it's a bluebird.
I propose a western scrub jay.
A kindergarten boy in my wife's class proves us all wrong.
His book of birds and eggs says:

Sage Thrasher.

Over the next week, the crop increases.
Updates for the keen Kindergarteners.
We all invested in the nest

                                        until

A night time robbery halves the number.
The parents are skittish in the tree.

Two days later and the nest is empty.
The parents paralyzed with loss.

The kindergarten students cry.
We all feel an emptying.

Easter Monday Circles

Over the Deschutes river near the Old
Mill, hundreds of tree swallows gather,
celebrating water and sun and chance
in endless tightening circles, part-panic,
part ballet. Above them circles a single
bald eagle, rising higher and heavenly,
wings written with feathered prayers,
to become spotted obscurity in blue,
angel to the waxing Moon smudging
the morning with its blink, taking turns
to encircle the hope. The eagle merges
with the moon, the swallows disperse,
and the river conducts the resurrection
song of sun and water and chance.

The Zen of a Garden Sprinkler

I saw my doppelganger
walking down a flight of
steps and suddenly cry out
as ten foot high sprinklers
blasted the bank, soaking
one entire side of his body.

In the cold April morning,
sun yawning over the Cascades,
I expected shouts and curses.
instead, he shook his head,
laughed, thanked the spray
for teaching humility, how
to find a rainbow in rain.

Three Teenagers on the Riverbank

Three teenagers stroll the Deschutes east bank,
rapid laughing, bursts of galloping and jostling,
comparing the mud on the hem of their jeans,
roaring with momentary outrages and running
to catch up with a strident, fatherly figure ahead.
A pair of buffleheads stop short, stare, swim on
while the three cubs scuff and claw their world.
The river sighs but forgives. It was young once,
just a glacier's first gift to the lava coated world,
in a hurry to prove the rumor of open oceans.
The teenagers disappear into myth, their music
still stinging the silenced warblers. A great blue
heron appears with a prehistoric cry and takes
flight to a nearby tree where it stands sentinel.

Three Puddles

Giggling with permission
the little Goldilocks sniggers
up to the first of three puddles.

She stamps on the first small one.
Not enough
splash.

She skips to the second and kicks.
Not enough wash over the wellies.

She sneaks up to the big one.
Now she jumps and shouts
and splashes the world
for this is the most fun she could have

and all the adults remember
when they had this much fun.
So they record her on their phones.

He Talks of His Wine

He talks of his wine, his children:
each has its merit, excuses
for locally strengthened characters.

I'm a good old country boy, really.
Just jeans and a neck scarf, see?
No fancy ski-set dress up here.

He talks about squalls over Roseburg,
the special soil of the Umpqua hills,
the unique grapes that flourish.

We mention the battle ground
of last summer's record forest fires,
accidently igniting a local conspiracy:

it was those ANTIFA arsonists
bored of fighting police in Portland,
they came to punish the forests.

I don't understand the thinking.
My whole life a local fire-fighter—
with some security work in Europe.

He recommends chocolate shops
how cranberries are harvested,
tempts us with fruit experiments.

We taste wines, sneaking sips
between masks. He doesn't wear one.
We take two of his children with us.

The Mole Crab

Bandon beach. An elderly woman
caged in a pink coat pokes exposed
soft shells and mechanical innards.

She calls out to ask what it all is.
We stand around hypothesizing:
prehistoric crab? Armored shrimp?

Feathery hems confuse us all.
She asks us to find out, tell her.
Her husband rolls his eyes.

The internet says: mole crab.
They live in the frothy surf,
flying little filament flags to catch

the drifting winds of plankton.
We see the woman on the way back.
Despite deafness, we inform her.

A few waves of gratitude and she
wanders off with husband to bury
herself back into our unknowing.

Whale Rock

Blasting of the rocking waves,
a suggestive hiss of volcanic steam—
the first sign. We point, wait...
has the long-feared earthquake arrived?

Then the surface of the sea cracks
open with gasps: surely this
is the seabed itself, thrusted
skyward by a tectonic fist

rolling around in the water
in a barnacled lump of softened
rock smoothed over centuries
of subjunctive rubbing. As quickly

as it rose, the seabed slice sinks
back down again to the bottom,
bubbling back into geology,
leaving a tsunami of wonderment.

Remains of Redwood

Near the storm-tossed tantrum
of trunks and bleached branches
that mustache the beach's upper lip
there grins a vast ghost-white base
between two huge rocks, confused
for a rock or a rejected coral reel.
But this is the core of a long vanished
mammoth swept down from California
by some infernal tempest, torn apart
and thrown fossilized onto the beach
long before there was Bandon, OR,
the forgetfulness of the white folk,
the settlers and the loggers robbing
the coast of its space and emptiness.

The Tree Swallows Return

I awaken from the nucleus of meditation
and find the space
filled with electrons, fired up in flight,
defined in moments of white,
that scoop and slide and slip
through all levels of being
down the river's potential.

That night, through a valley
in the tops of the pine trees,
they wink past in wrinkles
under the waxing eye of the moon.

The next day, the air clots
with eddying particles rejoicing
the return to the river.
They pirouette sharper than waves,
faster than currents.

They are both feather and water
until observed.

They rise up like a ballerina's circling hands.

Lava Butte Speaks

Don't waste time worrying
about the late Green Card,
shocking doctor's bills, trying
to be a good husband for her.

I will consume you in the end.
Even my smallest igneous grain
will outlast every one of your
hopes and dreams and gray hairs.

Look at that chipped necklace
of volcanos you call Cascades,
dormant only in human cycles.
Look at their shrinking glaciers,

the lessening snow, thirsting rivers.
Feel the unnaturally warm early
spring day you have all cooked up.
I will outlive even these changes.

The Bandon Labyrinth

We wander the heavenly golf course
following stone stained trails, searching
for the famous dunes. Appearing lost,
we were granted lifts by golfing gods.

A northwestern salamander stutters
across a damp woodland trail, a toddling
monster dazzled by its lumbering limbs.
We lose ourselves in the wood. March

beckons with mulch, winking gorse flowers,
dripping lichen and snatches of sunlight
between moistly rotting trees, collapsing
haphazardly on route to becoming soil.

We find a labyrinth modeled on Chartres.
Follow it around and around—no choices,
just patience and arriving at the center.
that's the meditative point only realized

when we leave.

Empire Barber

A travel tradition:
a haircut to honor the new place.
We still talk about how bad
the cut was in Reykjavik.

Passing through Coos Bay, OR,
my hair long and visibly gray,
we see 'Empire Barbers.'
My always-right wife insists.

Muffled by mask, my barber
is from northern Vietnam.
19 years in the US. Regularly returns
home, well, that was pre-COVID.
So very hot and humid in the summer.

We swap stories about living in south China.
Guangzhou—the factory of the world.
He knows all about that. People take
cheap stuff back to sell in Vietnam.

Has a sister in Germany.
Our old home, Dresden.
Florence of the Elbe. Dresden?
Been three times. You lived there?
Stops razoring often to guffaw in amazement.

He follows Man City football club
from Vietnam to Oregon.
We briefly watch a World Cup qualifier.
England beating San Marina 4-0.

I leave with better hair
and an improved soul,
my wife smiling like a Buddha.

Cape Lookout

We look but don't see any whales.

Instead we see the Pacific
as an upturned offering bowl from the heavens.

Comets current white lines that pass
close to the yellow start of infinity.

Dark matter pools in random places,
the invisible energy of tug and tear.

Pelicans shoot through the net of blue,
constellations of action and hunger.

Islands eject from the coast like still comets,
the sandy tail trailing south.

Tree sparrows star the cliff top
with their pointed wings.

We look but don't see any whales.

White Kafka Waits

white privilege
[wahyt-priv-uh-lij, priv-lij, hwahyt]

Noun:

Waiting for my Residency Card: emails politely asking me to wait 90 days (in my comfortable ADU rental in Bend), wait another 30 days, bored women on the phone in Texas telling me to wait longer, then emails unanswered, hours on the phone, finally told by more bored voices to go to the Immigration office in Portland (not a detention center) and ask them to work what's going on, queue with immigrants and their translators, unfriendly guards with dead eyes and sloppy bellies, *but why are you here?* explaining the whole story to an bemused Immigration Officer, pleading for him to help in my Mother Tongue, *Deferred Inspection* needed (not Title 42 enforcement), wife drives me in our newly purchased car to Hillsboro airport (not bussed to a different state in soulless Senatorial stunt) to confuse one more customs man in a tiny office who is unamused but efficient, exchanging smiles with a Brazilian family, waiting, waiting, suddenly the door opens, out comes Authority and passport given back—all done, sent off, I go, Green Card will come in a couple of weeks and I call this country 'home' without paying a Coyote, hiding in a trunk, barred from a plane, last seen as footsteps leading down the bank of a border river where there are too many tragic poems to read.

First Kiss

Bend Autumn Music & Art Festival.
The season's first public drunks,
arguing couples stomping streets,
artwork dreams exploring their depth,
children sniffing something for them.
The urgency of being back together.

Sudden firework of teenage girl voices.
The air crackles with cries as girls
in dark clothes and dyed hair run back
and forth, wailing like zealots. They
crowd, excited and then split. Screams
of parting, wanting to be heard. Two
pass by muttering. *Well, first kiss, pretty
gross.* Shoulders shrugged. *No big deal.*

The Pumpkin Field

Being just a poor British boy grown
where London's roots defile Saxon towns,
common woods and meadows, I know little
about agriculture beyond the shelves
and tin cans of childhood. So when I see

the field of pumpkins on the edge of I-5 North,
the bulbous fruit strung out like orange pearls
in finely tuned rows, small hard heads lolled
on the dry soil, I am amazed. That so much
can be gained from these ignorant seeds.

Midwinter Scenes, Pacific City, OR

My wife runs off down the beach,
a declining figure becoming a near
future worry. She runs southwards
where an arcing white whale marks
the Nestucca river fleeing into sea.

The waves cry out white manes
toppled by the charging of the high
tide breaching the lip of the beach.
A few seconds of ferocity flattened
out into a frothing line in the sand.

I stand by a fossilized spine spearing
the sand, darkened by a forgotten
forest, the storm-stripped trunk too
big to roll in the surf like other logs,
so lays a slowly rotting memorial.

Sanderlings play chase with the surf,
stabbing the just-wet sand until
new waves flurry them up the beach.
They scuttle back through fear,
robotic legs blur under white bellies.

A tired calligrapher paints drooping
lines of geese spelling northward.
White commas punctuate the space
around Cape Kiwanda's prehistoric
painted cliff. Clouds begin to clear.

The sun promises to dismiss cynics.
Midwinter exclaims another year.
The crescendoing percussion of waves
and surf sucking back on the sand.
The relief of my wife's returning line.

Cheated

Outside a Safeway, Starbucks in hand
wondering if there exists
places devoid of the poetic.

Car park tarmac.
Gloomy January evening.

Almost evidence

only there is a irregular puddle
of water into which
falls tampering rain drops
as if it was its own private cloud.

The Impossible Resident

Just when you thought you knew all their tricks.

An Anna's Hummingbird appears
outside the patio doors. It's winter

in White Salmon. The Columbia's clouds
disgorge over the rounded hills.

Everything is damp, empty, still except
for this tiny buzz of disbelief

searching all the doorsteps, gardens,
frosted feeders for food enough

to last until spring. This impossible resident
cajoling just enough calories.

Should snow spoil her search, she will take
to her tree post, hidden by bark

and tremble herself into torpor, heart slowed
while cozy relatives frolick south.

Joy in Others

I wish I was more like my in-laws.
They delight in people's company.
They set aside time like a forgotten
currency and spend it listening to
old friends, family, newly met people.
They listen and engulf the other,
applauding stories, rolling laughter,
making the other feel like their world.
The older they become, the more
they do this, the more I wish I could
make the other feel that vital, sacred.
But then I would have no time to think
words to express what is missing,
poems to offer in place of apologies.

Hunger On a Beach in Baja California Sur, Mexico

The sea-chewed remnants of life lay littered on the beachy gums of La Ventana beach. Toothed debris of wood and seaweed, bleached coral chunks and plastic mark the tidal smile line. Here lay scattered skeletons of fish: spinal columns, skulls agape with sharp teeth, the leathery, empty sacks of fish skins, discarded vertebrae; the resting place for tenants of the former Aquarium of the World. Always patrolling are the vultures, keen-eyed for any carrion. Two politely take turns tugging inside a fish head. Seagulls watch and snatch a lump when the vultures get bored and take to hungry wingtips, wind spitting them up to look-out posts. Suddenly an osprey in the air, ducking a seagull trying to steal the wriggling fish in its left claw. It disappears, fish still squirming. A squadron of pelicans glide over the water, bellies touching down on gentle waves. They sit watching on the water with huge bills lowered like mourners. A few frigates arrive, painting black patient lines with forked winds and split tails. Pacific wanderers hanging on the breeze with origami wings cut like kites, above endless waves, constant hunger, smiles and grimaces.

The Eel

It's always a lion or a tiger
eagles for empires, predatory,
top of the food chain. Ask me

six months ago, I'd pick the eel
that master of reinvention
made in Caribbean disbelief

and wriggled through mystery
halfway across the world,
held in purpose four times,

each discarded, no hesitation.
Now I am here in Oregon,
I am lost in my own Sargasso.

wondering where the eel mates,
what wheels it across the world,
from salt to fresh to saltwater,

how they find their way home.
No obstacle on earth can deter
shape-shifters in the currents.

But I am tired of transforming.
My heart is a hummingbird,
but my body wants to be sloth.

Quintessence

Awaiting a delayed parent
after the Grade 6 rehearsal of Hamlet,
I direct a student to what seems a star
but is in fact Jupiter, Lord of the Solar System.

On the other side of the pine shines
Venus, Lady of the Early Evening
as bright as a plane light, but motionless,
tempting diamond comparisons.

In between the stretched out triangle,
pricks Saturn, sneaking into view.

The student says it's cool and means it,
I think.

We stare into infinite space for a few seconds,
two piles of dust not bound by nutshells.
I hear Polonius tutting—no telescope.
His boy would be better advised.

Our minds both a little nobler, but think
what could be achieved if every young
quintessence of dust could look
                    up from screens
                                    to be.

Old Mill at Night

Riding home late at night with my wife.

The river shimmers
with a nearly full moon

held between the two exclamations
of the Old Mill's redundant lumber chimneys.

We ride
former full moons in other countries
and thank
the river for carrying us

here.

www.ingramcontent.com/pod-product-compliance
Lightning Source LLC
Chambersburg PA
CBHW020222090426
42734CB00008B/1176